PER KIRKEBY

WITHDRAWN

709.2 KLR

D1493682

PER KIRKEBY

Jill Lloyd

Tate Gallery Publishing

Sponsored by Coutts Group

Coutts

Supported by the Danish
Contemporary Art Foundation

DANISH CONTEMPORARY ART FOUNDATION

Published by order of the Trustees
of the Tate Gallery 1997
by Tate Gallery Publishing Ltd
Millbank, London SW1P 4RG
© Tate Gallery 1998

ISBN 185437 266 1

This catalogue is published to accom-
pany the exhibition at the Tate Gallery
3 February – 26 May 1998

A catalogue record for this book is
available from the British Library

Designed and typeset by
Martin Brown

Printed and bound in Great Britain
by M&TJ Print Limited

Frontispiece: Per Kirkeby in his studio
in Copenhagen, 1997, photograph by
Hugo Glendinning

Contents

Director's Foreword

Per Kirkeby is one of Denmark's leading contemporary artists. His original training was in geology which took him to many parts of the world including Central America and Greenland and these experiences have inspired his work. Although his work is well known in the rest of Europe, he has shown only occasionally in this country, the most substantial exhibition being as long ago as 1985. We are delighted that he responded so positively to our invitation to create an installation for the Tate's Duveen Galleries. His enthusiasm for this project was partly due to the challenge of the space but also because of his great love for Turner. Indeed one of the paintings in the exhibition relates closely to Turner's *Fall of an Avalanche* (fig.1) which is on view in the Clore Gallery.

Kirkeby works in a variety of other media including film, performance and poetry. However, in this exhibition he has chosen to limit himself to three specific groups of works: large bronze sculptures, large abstract paintings, and small models for larger architectural works. In addition, he has created a new brick sculpture, one of his 'buildings with no function', examples of which can be found on public sites in many European cities. This new work runs the length of the North Duveen, splitting the gallery in two and deliberately impeding the discovery of the paintings, each placed in one of the six bays along the sides of the gallery.

Michael Werner of Galerie Michael Werner, Cologne and New York, and his colleagues Erika Költzsch and Angeline Enderlein have been unfailingly helpful and their generous support and advice is deeply appreciated.

In 1996 Per Kirkeby was awarded the Coutts Contemporary Art Award and Coutts Group has generously supported this exhibition. We have also received a donation from the Danish Contemporary Art Foundation. We offer them both our sincere thanks.

Per Kirkeby designed the new brick sculpture specially for the exhibition. This work could not have been realised without help from a number of sources. First I should like to thank Ibstock Building Products Limited, and in particular Susan Waldrum and Jamie Pickles, which has generously supplied the bricks. BRC Products Ltd through Suzanne Pugh has provided the reinforcement material necessary for the sculpture. Andrew Hickin of Masonry Projects Services Limited has advised us about the installation of the piece and secured the bricklayers, mortar and scaffolding. We are deeply grateful to them all for their willingness to collaborate on this project and for their generosity.

Finally we owe our deep gratitude to the artist himself. He has devoted a considerable amount of time to many aspects of the project and has been closely involved with the installation. We have much enjoyed working with him to realise this exhibition.

Nicholas Serota
Director

Sponsor's Foreword

Coutts Group is delighted to be sponsoring the Tate Gallery's Per Kirkeby exhibition.

In 1992 the Coutts Contemporary Art Foundation was founded as part of Coutts & Co's tercentenary celebrations. The aim of the foundation is to benefit artists in the forefront of development in the visual arts by making biennial awards.

Per Kirkeby was a recipient of a 1996 award and we are pleased to be continuing our involvement with him.

Coutts Group is the international private banking arm of the NatWest Group, one of the world's leading providers of financial services, and serves clients around the world.

Coutts' international private banking clients are wealthy individuals who have complex financial needs over their lifetime. Coutts provides tailored and integrated services to manage their wealth. High quality, personal service is at the core of Coutts' operations.

Sir Ewen Fergusson GCMG, GCVO
Chairman, Coutts Group &
Coutts Contemporary Art Foundation

Supporter's Foreword

The Danish Contemporary Art Foundation is delighted to support the Tate Gallery's exhibition of Danish painter Per Kirkeby.

The Danish Contemporary Art Foundation is an independent institution established by the Ministry of Culture in 1995. Its mission is to promote an ongoing dialogue between Danish and international contemporary art. Its activities comprise support of Danish artists abroad and of international artists in Denmark, involvement in important international exhibitions, establishing

exhibition possibilities and studio programmes, as well as information and publication activities.

It is with great pleasure and pride that we are now able to support this important presentation of Per Kirkeby's work which will no doubt find a large audience within the British public to whom this magnificent Danish artist of international standards is still not very well known.

Lars Grambye
Director

1 J.M.W. Turner, *Fall of an Avalanche in the Grisons*, exhibited 1810
Oil on canvas 90.2 x 120 cm. Tate Gallery

Per Kirkeby: the Marriage of Grief and Reason

Per Kirkeby's recent paintings, hanging in counterpoint to his brick and bronze sculptures in the present exhibition, herald a new departure. Glowing colours, like the vermilions and lapis lazulis in *The Siege of Constantinople* (pl. 5), make up rich mosaics of form which are more consciously artificial than in Kirkeby's previous work and less redolent of nature. Lit by a blinding light and divided by a rift of shadow, the rock formations in *Withdrawn from the World* (pl. 8) are drawn from stylized mountains in the backgrounds of Byzantine and medieval manuscript paintings that Kirkeby admires. But the tumbling rocks in *Untitled*, 1997 (pl. 7) are less a rendition of nature than a direct variation on a painting of the same subject by Turner (fig. 1), who remains one of Kirkeby's most vital sources of inspiration. Turner, Kirkeby explains, 'always goes beyond the boundaries of good taste'. And, more recently, 'Turner's paintings are totally artificial.'[1]

Over the past two or three years, as Kirkeby approaches his sixtieth birthday, he has also become preoccupied by the late work of artists he admires like Edvard Munch and Kurt Schwitters. His subjects in the most recent paintings have to do with violent ruptures and transformations in western civilization: the breaking apart of the Byzantine Empire, or the moment of utter desolation in the landscape that reflects Christ's agony on the cross: '"My God, my God, why hast thou forsaken me?"...And, behold, the veil of the temple was rent in twain, and the earth did quake, and the rocks rent; And the graves were opened.'

Kirkeby's religious references are new; but on an underlying level his recent paintings are deeply rooted in his past. With his diverse range of activities as a film-maker, explorer, poet, gifted critic and architect, Kirkeby can seem a difficult artist to pin down. The sensual paintings, which remain his central, most important activity, and the conceptual sculptures in brick, seem at first sight to come from opposite ends of the aesthetic spectrum. And yet the same issues, which have become increasingly focused in recent years, recur in all the mediums. 'Whatever the material... it comes back to the same thing,' Kirkeby writes, 'but this is very difficult to define because it is precisely what makes up my work.'[2]

The origins of Kirkeby's intuitive, poetic philosophy date back to his student years in Copenhagen in the 1950s. Today Kirkeby is one of the most erudite artists on the contemporary scene with an extensive understanding of art history as well as many other branches of knowledge. But his art is essentially autodidactic. Although Kirkeby painted and drew throughout his childhood, he chose in 1957 to study geology at Copenhagen University rather than enter the Academy because of the sterile, retrogressive nature of the teaching there. His early training in the methodology of the natural sciences and, above all, his unforgettable experiences of the Arctic landscape during student expeditions to Peary Land and Melville Bay in Greenland between 1958 and 1963, underlie all his later work. Kirkeby recorded his impressions of the Arctic zone in drawings, diaries and prints and still frequently alludes to the existential loneliness he felt when faced by empty expanses of light and snow: 'You're about as alone as you can be on this earth up there – with no company but the moon. You feel that you can somehow be swallowed up or disappear in the landscape.'[3]

Later, this primal, anonymous landscape, beyond time and place, which is both a threat and, in a certain sense, a liberation, became one of the ingredients of Kirkeby's complex meditations on nature. At the time, however, his expeditions fed directly into performances like *Arctic 1–3*, which he staged as a member of the Experimental Art School in Copenhagen. Founded in 1961 as an alternative to the Academy, this unofficial school soon became a focus for Scandinavian artists participating in Fluxus, Happenings, Pop Art and Minimalism. Kirkeby first met Joseph Beuys when he came to Copenhagen to perform *The Chief* in 1964, and he participated in Fluxus events in the mid-sixties organized by George Maciunas in Germany and New York. At the same time, he continued to paint, although he remembers how difficult it was to assert his 'right' to do so in the experimental atmosphere of the sixties. To compromise between his own impulses and the demands of Minimalism, he began around 1963 to paint on square masonite panels which could be arranged in series on the wall to form an interchangeable, repeating pattern.

This method of containing the subjective act of painting, which involved a mixture of gestural brushwork and collage, within a strictly disciplined and objectifying framework, initiated a practice which was to have lasting consequences for Kirkeby. Very soon afterwards the first of his sculptures, consisting of a simple square block made up of eighteen bricks, resulted from a similar desire to combine opposing forces. Brick was a local, vernacular material which sparked off a series of memories and associations for Kirkeby. His early childhood had been spent in a brick council house built as part of the social housing complex around Grundtvig Church in Copenhagen (fig. 2). This vast, monumental brick church in neo-gothic style was an awe-inspiring presence that later became associated in Kirkeby's imagination with the classicism of Boullée and Ledoux and the crystalline architecture of Expressionists like Poelzig, Scharoun and Bruno Taut. By using a material that was charged with personal, local and historical associations in a strictly objective serial structure, Kirkeby was able to forge his own subjective, poetic version of the international Minimalist style.

Looking back on the sixties in his *Notes on Happenings*, Kirkeby remembers a period of 'border crossings', 'entropy', 'hybrid forms', 'violent mutations' and 'transgressions'. By the end of this period he felt that he had reached, like the French novelist Alain Robbe-Grillet, a 'zero-point existence' and won his way through to a new freedom. His ability to traverse the boundaries that traditionally separate literature, painting and science certainly relate to 'this era of everything' when many of his fellow artists in Copenhagen were experimenting across these divides. Asger Jorn who, like Kirkeby, was a talented writer, also became a model for this aspect of his work. Kirkeby's oblique, poetic way of thinking, which feeds directly into his paintings, often results from making associations or transferring concepts from one discipline to another in order to come up with his own subjective reinterpretations of established facts.

2 Façade of the Grundtvig Church, Copenhagen. Photo James Bellamy/ Architectural Association

This can be seen in the next formative experience which, as so often in Kirkeby's life, involved a physical and imaginative voyage. In 1971 he joined an expedition to Central America, where he was deeply moved and impressed by the remains of Mayan culture he encountered. Kirkeby acted as the expedition's draughtsman (fig. 3), drawing, writing and filming to record, as his fellow-traveller, the novelist Ib Michael, later recalled, 'those strange visions which the Maya country transmits to Western minds, arising in the no-man's land between ruin, monument and hieroglyph.'[4] In many different ways Kirkeby's experiences of visiting 'the forsaken Mayan cities... and the ancient high places' shaped his ideas and attitudes. The Mayan ruins, which were resonant of religious ceremonies but no longer functioning as temples, appeared to him as sculptures, and it was here that the idea evolved of placing large, public sculptures in relation to a particular setting. At the same time the carved figures he saw, like the Olmec sculptures in Mexico, convinced him that a fragment of the human body

with 'a lower face broken off, a missing arm' is 'just as full of expression as the thing itself'.[5] It was almost as if the fragmentation and damage that the sculptures had suffered – signs of the passage of time – made the surviving concept of the whole figure more unique and meaningful than it was in its original state.

The really crucial development for Kirkeby in Mexico, however, was his new attitude to landscape. In Greenland, where he had gone as a geologist, he had experienced a primal, absolute landscape. But in Mexico, where he witnessed the ancient Mayan ruins being reclaimed by the rain forests, he became aware of a historical, temporal landscape as well. With his habit of eliding the languages of different disciplines, Kirkeby immediately recognized a relationship between the layerings of geology and archaeology. Both could be described as the 'reason' lying behind the surface of nature and of architecture. Moreover, in Kirkeby's mind, the fundamental 'reason' or 'cause' of architecture, which is expressed in shapes like cones, pyramids and boxes, also existed as the structure underlying nature.[6]

During the first half of the seventies, Kirkeby continued his travels (to the Central Asian republics, to Greenland, to Turkey) and made several films, including an epic feature on the Vikings and a documentary on Asger Jorn. This was a fertile period in which several strands of his development came together. Although Kirkeby was committed to painting by this date, his experiments in the sixties had convinced him that paintings could not be made in a direct, unreflective way. 'Sincerity means moving in circles', he wrote in 1975. 'Expression, art must not be sincerity. Art is tricks. Art is not psychology.'[7] Like other artists of his generation, notably Sigmar Polke, Kirkeby was impressed by Picabia's anarchic use of kitsch and popular images alongside quotes from the great masterpieces of western painting. Just before he left for Mexico, Kirkeby had begun to use tracings and stencils of fashion plates in his paintings (for example, fig. 4) together with popular images like the covers from Tintin's *Travels Across the World*. By the mid-seventies he also used overhead projections of his own drawings or illustrations from a volume of natural science or art history, which he would trace onto his paintings in order to avoid becoming 'too involved' in their surfaces.

12

3 Kirkeby sketching in Uxmal, Mexico, photographed by Teit Jorgensen.

4 Per Kirkeby *The Murder in Finnerup Lade*, 1967.
122 x 122 cm. Galerie Michael Werner (photo Lars Bay).

All these elements became components of what Kirkeby calls his 'pornographic' or impure landscape paintings, which he began in the early seventies and continues to this day. But only glimpses of images remain in the finished works, through layers of colour that the artist applies over a long period of time. Kirkeby says that he always begins painting with a motif in mind (a figure, a tree, a landscape), but that very soon the inner dynamic of painting takes on a life of its own. Using, as he often does, language originally associated with geology, he has described his paintings as 'a summing-up of structures; a sedimentation of thin, thin layers'.[8] Kirkeby also superimposes motifs drawn from nature – leaves, trees, stones and waves – to create complex patterns. Applying colours with a brush and a palette knife, he sets up a dialogue between spontaneous marks and deliberately countered spontaneity. Each touch is adjusted in relation to its surroundings, and the traces of images that remain at the end of this long process flicker in and out of focus, emerging, only to fade once again into pure strokes of colour.

Kirkeby has compared his method of painting to a long journey when new impressions constantly crowd in. The ornamental tattoos that he sometimes inscribes onto his surfaces, which were originally inspired by the decorative motifs he found in Mayan artefacts, are part of the complex process he has evolved of setting off one type of mark or layer of imagery against another. But these ornaments on the surface of his paintings also relate to the issue of finish. Kirkeby long admired Gustave Moreau and regarded the linear tattoos he applied to his paintings as a sign of the artist's impulse to finish a work that was constantly defeated by the assertive presence of underlying layers of paint. Kirkeby feels that his paintings are finished when the motif or sensation that obsessed him at the outset reappears in a different and unexpected guise and, in this sense, the paintings involve an existential act of losing himself in order to find his way. In every finished work the motif has undergone a death and a resurrection in the artist's attempt to uncover – through the paradoxical process of layering and covering up – an underlying and truer sense of reality.

Kirkeby's method of layering and working in series relates to his awareness that the landscape is not only a space but also a harbinger of time. Although his paintings rarely focus on a particular sense of place, they often evoke the changing seasons and are charged with memories and associations (pl. 2). Ever since the mid-seventies, his recognition of the transitoriness and relativity of the landscape has been expressed through his use of colour to evoke light. Kirkeby indeed describes colour as 'a nameless light-bearing substance'[9] (pl. 1), and he is acutely aware of how the mood of the landscape changes when it is illuminated by a sudden shaft of light or plunged into shadow. Exact nuances of colour tend to be determined by psychological and emotional states: 'the sunset on the evening my first wife kicked me out', Kirkeby explains, is 'a different kind of sunset and the colours are not orange and green but very special colours with no names'.[10] Like his great Scandinavian precursor, Edvard Munch, Kirkeby views the landscape as a reflection of the human condition and for all the sensuality of his paintings they remain conceptual in the sense that they are, as Kirkeby puts it, 'something to think in', 'a place for your soul and not just for the splendour of nature'.[11]

5 A. Rodin, *The Gates of Hell*, Bronze. Height 635 cm Musée Rodin (photo Erik and Petra Hesmerg).

'Landscapes', Kirkeby has stated elsewhere, 'are about beauty and death. The only way you can define beauty – in a tree, for instance – is to know that death is hiding behind it'.[12] Underlying the relativity and temporality of Kirkeby's landscapes there is always a sense of something impenetrable, even confrontational, that recalls his descriptions of the primal, Arctic landscape of snow and ice he encountered as a student. This extreme landscape surfaces in the earthquakes, avalanches and geological rifts that appear so frequently in his recent work. But it is also there in a less obvious sense as part of the spatial experience of all Kirkeby's work. The paintings are, in the end, wall-like structures that repel the viewer's attempts to enter their space. Kirkeby recognizes this when he describes the paintings as 'carpet' or 'wallpaper'... 'it is a carpet when the repoussoirs push in from all sides, with no regard for up or down. It is wallpaper when they go down over the picture like a roller-blind'.[13]

Among Kirkeby's many perceptive works of art criticism, his essay on Rodin's *Gates of Hell* (fig. 5) is a key to understanding his own oeuvre. Although Kirkeby is describing Rodin's epic sculpture in the following extract, it could easily be read as a characterization of the aesthetic principles operating in his paintings: '...Through the whole thing go fractures and geological faults. Above all concentrated in the mullions and frame mouldings...here lies the tectonic drama. The great and eternal movement that lies under the surface of the globe, under our lives, which is there even if periods look regular and symmetrical on the surface...the movement beneath us released in leaps, in fractures, in what geologists read as faults... The *Gates* are in reality several crosses placed at different depths. Several crosses naturally give middleground. Middleground that is at the same time background. A background that is not a prospect. It is closed, the space walled up. It teems with confusion. Impossible really to get hold of what is happening in these fields'.[14]

Kirkeby also acknowledges an underlying affinity with Rodin in his own sculptural work, which has always been a parallel activity to his painting, but which has become increasingly important since the early eighties when the artist began to cast his small clay models in bronze. These models are conceived in an intuitive way and are, in this sense, closest to his paintings. They are correspondances rather than exact models for the large brick sculptures, and Kirkeby uses them to develop forms and proportions and to work out the relationships between volumes, between mass and space, contours and planes (figs. 6, 7).

6a *Model for Mönchengladback*, 1985 (no.12)

6b *Model*, 1993 (no.31)

6c *Model for Amsterdam*, 1989 (no.15)

6d *Model for Antwerp*, 1992 (no.26)

6e *Model for Vevey*, 1990 (no.17)

Fig.6 Per Kirkeby. Bronze Models
For a full caption see List of Exhibited
Works, page 31.

Fig.7 Per Kirkeby. Bronze Models
For a full caption see List of Exhibited
Works, page 31.

7a *Model for Rijksmuseum Kröller Müller,
Otterlo* 1987 (no.13)

7b *Model for Bremen,* 1988 (no.14)

7c *Model for València,* 1989 (no.16)

7d *Model,* 1990 (no.18)

7e *Model for Års,* 1990 (no.19)

7f *2nd Design Groningen,* ca. 1990 (no.20)

7g *Model*, 1990 (no.21)

7h *Model*, 1990 (no.22)

7i *Model*, 1991 (no.24)

7j *Model for Nakskov*, 1991 (no.23)

7k *Model for Paderborn*, 1992 (no.25)

7l *Model for Nordland*, 1992 (no.27)

7m *Model for Göppingen*, 1992 (no.28)

7n *Model for Ballerup*, 1992 (no.29)

7o *Model*, 1993 (no.30)

In an interview at the beginning of the nineties, Kirkeby remarked how Rodin and Giacometti realized that 'questions of proportion are not simply an aesthetic issue.' It is necessary, he continued, to 'measure yourself against the proportions of the sculpture'.[15] Kirkeby's larger bronze sculptures are meditations on the human body and on the relationships between body and space. His preoccupation with fragments of bodies – *Two Arms, Head and Arm, Large Nose* (figs 8, 9, 10) – was originally inspired by the fractured temple sculptures that he discovered in Mexico. But a more important influence was 'the radicalizing of the torso' he experienced in Rodin's work. In Rodin's figure studies for *The Gates of Hell* Kirkeby found that 'an arm or leg or some other limb becomes a whole body'.[16] Just as palaeontology, which was one of the great enthusiasms of Rodin's day, demonstrates how a fossil bone from a dinosaur can be viewed as 'a thing in itself', so too

do Rodin's body fragments appear complete. To experience this new sense of the body, Rodin, in Kirkeby's view, exaggerates forms and embraces 'the explosion tearing the limbs from each other...dispersed limbs that in their severed state gather themselves into a synthetic effort of strength.' This results in new monumental forms like *Balzac*, which Kirkeby considers one of Rodin's most successful sculptures and which he reads as 'an arm that has become a figure'.[17]

Much depends, in this new vision of the human body, on Rodin's treatment of surface, and this applies in equal measure to Kirkeby's own modelling of the surfaces of his sculptures in bronze. Both artists model in terms of what Kirkeby calls 'bandages of material which is light',[18] allowing us to experience the body in a state of constant transformation and

interchange with its surroundings. The explosion that tears the part from the whole (which is like a geological event at the heart of the universe) and the dissolution of form into light are not ends in themselves, but rather a means of reinventing what Kirkeby calls 'the statuesque.' 'Far beneath the undefined surface, the flowing transition between mass and surroundings' he explains, 'the molecules are condensed into a firm structure'.[19] Falling apart (as if in the wake of a rift or an avalanche) is also a condition of the work of art pulling together into a new poetic reality. In this sense the methods and aims behind Kirkeby's paintings and his sculptures are very close indeed.

8 Per Kirkeby *Two Arms*, 1984.

9 Per Kirkeby *Head and Arm*, 1984.

10 Per Kirkeby *Large Nose*, 1984.

11 Per Kirkeby   Early brick construction in the Kunsthalle, Berne.

12 Per Kirkeby   Public Sculpture at Ballerup 1996, photographed by Jens Lindhe

The large, public sculptures in brick have their roots in the romantic minimalism that Kirkeby evolved in the sixties. Among his early constructions in brick was the tower-like structure now in the Kunsthalle, Berne (fig. 11), which was directly inspired by the Mayan temples Kirkeby saw in Mexico and experienced as sculptures rather than as buildings. By the early eighties, however, the archetypal, minimal, abstracted forms of the brick sculptures related more closely to Byzantine architecture, which had made a deep impression on Kirkeby when he visited Turkey in 1977. Memories of the early Christian buildings he prefers, like 'the old city walls of Constantinople... and some of the lesser churches like the one named Chora'[20] reverberated through the brick sculptures before references to Byzantine and Medieval art began to filter through in Kirkeby's paintings. Over the years he has become a great expert on Early Christian art which he regards as the foundation upon which the whole history of Western civilization rests, like an underlying geological stratum.

On a formal level, Kirkeby's search for universal, underlying values is expressed in his use of a limited number of geometric shapes and groundplans in the brick sculptures, like the cross or the labyrinth. This latter shape determines the form of the high wall built by Kirkeby down the centre of the Tate's sculpture gallery for his 1998 exhibition, and it is based on his sketches of the double helix, the figure that makes up the DNA molecule. Although these universal forms obviously have symbolic and associative meanings, they are objectified and rationalized by the strict formal order and anonymity of the brick sculptures. In this sense they are crystalline structures, rising up vertically as towers or spreading out horizontally across the ground. In recent years, when Kirkeby has also worked on several fully-fledged architectural projects, the brick sculptures also relate more closely to built structures, with walls and openings creating inner spaces (fig. 12).

When he is talking about his brick sculptures, Kirkeby often returns to the example of Grundtvig Church and the brick houses where he spent his early childhood. Although his parents lived in a house near to the neo-gothic church, Kirkeby spent much of his childhood in the real medieval city of Elsinor, where his grandparents dwelt 'in the shadow of the cathedral.' This experience of authentic medieval buildings served to highlight the artificiality of Grundtvig which,

despite its function as a church, has an exaggerated, almost caricatural form which goes beyond the necessity of function. This makes it comparable to Malevich's "architectones" which were often a subject of discussion at the Experimental Art School in Copenhagen in the sixties.[21]

The idea of a form that goes beyond the dictates of function also applies to Kirkeby's brick works. Obviously, the artist sets up a visual and conceptual dialogue with architecture, but this only serves to highlight the irrational, non-functional nature of the sculpture. There is also, once again, a tension between the fragment and the whole as the sculptures are like quotations of architecture. Like the bronze torsos, these quotations are endowed with a monumantality that forces us to reconsider our ideas about completeness and finish. The brick sculptures are, in a sense, the fullest expression of the new 'statuesqueness' Kirkeby desires and which could also be described as the underlying, poetic and truer sense of reality he aspires to give form to in all his art. Kirkeby associates this with a particular definition of classicism that he has formulated in relation to late works by the nineteenth-century

13 Bertel Thorvaldsen *Hercules*, 1843. Original plaster model. Height 388 cm. Thorvaldsen Museum, Copenhagen (photo Ole Woldby)

Danish sculptor, Bertel Thorvaldsen. Describing Thorvaldsen's aspirations in works like *Hercules* (fig 13), Kirkeby refers to 'the most powerful and pure attempt to reorganize life according to the principles of art. A profound re-organization which reaches far beyond the usual meaning of the word'.[22] What Kirkeby values in Thorvaldsen's classicism is the grandeur and the striving for an ideal dimension which also takes account of blindness and despair at ever achieving its goal.

Joseph Brodsky, the great late-twentieth-century poet, also wrote about grandeur and despair when he described the ingredients of Robert Frost's poetry as 'grief and reason, which, while poison to each other, are language's most efficient fuel – or, if you will, poetry's indelible ink...The more one dips into it (the ink), the more it brims with this black essence of existence, and the more one's mind, like one's fingers, gets soiled by this liquid. For the more there is of grief, the more there is of reason... In Home Burial... while the characters stand, respectively, for reason and for grief, the narrator stands for their fusion. To put it differently, while the characters' actual union disintegrates, the story, as it were, marries grief to reason, since the bond of the narrative here supersedes the individual dynamics... the poem, in other words, plays fate'.[23]

Per Kirkeby, the poet, the painter, the sculptor, is also the narrator of his oeuvre. Over the entire range of his work he too combines grief and reason, order and chaos, in order to show reality in a new poetic perspective that allows us to see deeper into the nature of things. 'I use,' he explains, 'the brick sculptures to refer to the classicism that is also present in the works that bear the sign of my hand, and to keep hold of this anonymity. And I use the hand-made works to keep hold of the intuition and belief that resides in the brick sculptures'.[24]

Darkness and shadow, 'the black essence of existence,' are an element in Kirkeby's poetic transformation of the world, playing across the surfaces of his paintings and bronze sculptures and slicing through the niches in his brick works like black lines of 'darker air'.[25] But the more important, revolutionary force is light, which illuminates the colours in his most recent paintings with a new intensity and brilliance. 'When you have confronted your own shadow,' Kirkeby recently confided in conversation, 'you are able to go forward with new freedom.'[26] The religious references in his latest work have nothing to do with the established church, which Kirkeby regards as a social convention. They are there because the artist finds himself preoccupied by the magical authenticity he experiences in Early Christian art; and because the process of facing up to his own age and the prospect of death has made him look again at the story of Christ. '"My God, My God, why hast thou for-saken me?" That's where his (Jesus's) crisis begins, because he discovers that nothing lasts any more, there is no support...he carried out what is called ego-death, and he came out of it as himself...Darkness into light, that is Jesus emerging from the hole.'[27]

Kirkeby's interpretation of the medieval art and architecture he admires is as singular as his under-standing of classicism. In a recent comment about the Gothic cathedral in Strasbourg he explains how 'this idea of Gothic mysticism often seems to me banal and blind. I don't see anything mystical in it. On the con-trary, I see it as absolutely crystal clear, but it is reaching upwards towards something grand and experi-mental. I see something around which, like in all cases where structures are very audacious and very expressive, there floats the illuminated gas of transformation...'. Returning to the familiar theme of Grundtvig Church, he remarks on how its facade is also like an organic crystal, growing upwards. 'And my work is just like this too. An ascension, step by step, in order to constantly fall down again; a ladder with steps, like the gables of Grundtvig Church, with crystal steps that reach up towards the sky.'[28]

Jill Lloyd.

Footnotes

1 Michael Peppiatt, Interview with Per Kirkeby, *Art International* 14, Spring 1991 p.48 and in conversation with the author, November 6, 1997.

2 Philip Eddy Devolder, Interview with Per Kirkeby, exhib. cat. Galerie Phillippe Guimot, Brussels 1991.

3 Michael Peppiatt op. cit. p.45.

4 Ib Michael, 'The Jade Head', *Art International* 14, 1991 p.50.

5 Per Kirkeby, 'Mr Catherwood's Knife', English transl. in Per Kirkeby, *Pinturas, esculturas, grabados y escritos* exhib. cat. IVAM Centre del Carme, Valencia, Dec. 1989 – Feb. 1990 p.250.

6 Ibid p.254.

7 Per Kirkeby, 'A Selection of Images', see Per Kirkeby, *Early Works*, Gallerie Michael Werner, 1994

8 Per Kirkeby, 'Without a Parasol', IVAM 1989 – 90, op. cit. p.261.

9 Per Kirkeby, 'The Gate', IVAM 1989 – 90, op. cit. p. 270.

10 Michael Peppiatt, op. cit. p.45.

11 Per Kirkeby, 'Mr Catherwood's Knife and Flies', IVAM 1989 – 90, op. cit. p.254, 256.

12 Michael Peppiatt, op. cit. p.45.

13 Per Kirkeby, 'Without a Parasol', IVAM 1989 – 90, op. cit. p.264.

14 Per Kirkeby, 'The Gate', IVAM op. cit. p.268.

15 Michael Peppiatt, op. cit. p.48.

16 Per Kirkeby, 'The Gate', IVAMop. cit. p.268.

17 Ibid pp.269–270.

18 Ibid.

19 Ibid.

20 Lars Morell, *Per Kirkeby Baukunst*, 1996, p.246.

21 Per Kirkeby, 'Autour de l'église Grundtvig' in *Per Kirkeby*, exhib. cat. Musée des Beaux-Arts, Nantes 1995, p.56.

22 Musée des Beaux-Arts, Nantes, op. cit., p.17.

23 Joseph Brodsky, *On Grief and Reason*, London 1996 p.223f.

24 Per Kirkeby, *Von hier aus*, exhib. cat. Düsseldorf 1984, p.182.

25 Per Kirkeby, *Baukunst*, op. cit. p.286.

26 Interview with the author, November 6, 1997.

27 Per Kirkeby, *Baukunst*, op. cit. p.322.

28 Musée des Beaux-Arts, Nantes, op. cit. p.12.

Bibliography

Per Kirkeby: Paintings, sculpture, films (text Troels Andersen). Fruitmarket Gallery, Edinburgh, 1985

Per Kirkeby: Recent Painting and Sculpture (texts Tony Godfrey, Per Kirkeby), Whitechapel Art Gallery, London 1985–86

Per Kirkeby: Gemälde-Handzeichnungen-Skulpturen (texts Siegfried Gohr, Peter Schjedal, Troels Andersen, Andreas Franzke), Museum Ludwig, Cologne 1987

Per Kirkeby: Werke 1983–1988 (Texts Max Weschsler, Per Kirkeby), Kunstmuseum Winterthur, 1989

Per Kirkeby: Pinturas, esculturas, grabados y escritos (texts by Per Kirkeby in English), IVAM, Centre del Carme, Valencia, 1989–90

Per Kirkeby (texts Éric Darragon, Per Kirkeby) Musée des Beaux-Arts, Nantes, 1995

Michael Peppiatt: Interview with Per Kirkeby, *Art International* 14, Spring/Summer 1991

Per Kirkeby Early Works, Michael Werner Gallery, Cologne–New York, 1994

Per Kirkeby: Brickworks (text Lars Morell) 1996

Selected one-man exhibitions

1964
Exhibition of drawings and collages, Hoved Library, Copenhagen

1965
First one-man exhibition in Den Frie Udstillingsbygning, Copenhagen

1968
Jysk Kunstgalerie, Copenhagen;
Fyns Stiftsmuseum, Odense

1974
Michael Werner Gallery, Cologne

1975
Royal Museum of Fine Art, Copenhagen;
Henie-Onstad Kunstsenter, Hovikodden

1977
Museum Folkwang, Essen

1979
Kunsthalle Bern, Berne;
Kunstmuseum Aarhus

1982
Stedelijk Van Abbe Museum, Eindhoven

1984
Michael Werner Gallery, Cologne;
Kunstverein Braunschweig

1985
The Fruitmarket Gallery, Edinburgh;
Douglas Hyde Gallery, Dublin;
Den Frie Udstillingsbygning, Copenhagen;
Whitechapel Art Gallery, London

1986
Michael Werner Gallery, Cologne;
Städtisches Museum Abteiberg, Mönchengladbach

1987
Museum Ludwig, Cologne;
Museum Boymans-van Beuningeng, Rotterdam

1988
Michael Werner Gallery, Cologne

1989
Kunstmuseum Winterthur

1989/90
IVAM Centre del Carme, Valencia

1990
Städelsches Kunstinstitut, Frankfurt/Main;
Louisiana Museum of Modern Art, Humlebaek;
Michael Werner Gallery, Cologne

1991
Kunstmuseet Trapholt, Kolding

1991/92
Kestner Gesellschaft, Hannover;
MIT List Visual Arts Center, Cambridge (MA)

1992
Centre National d'Art Contemporain de Grenoble;
Parrish Art Museum, Southampton (NY);
Göteborgs Konstmuseum

1993
Kunstmuseet Koge Skitsesamling traveled;
Skissernas Museum, Lund;
Moderna galerija, Ljubljana

1994
Kunsthalle Recklinghausen;
National Gallery in Prague, Palais Sternberk

1995
Michael Werner Gallery, Cologne;
Musée des Beaux Arts de Nantes;
Openluchtmuseum voor Beeldehouwkunst Middelheim, Antwerp

1996
Michael Werner Gallery, New York;
Stadtgalerie Sundern;
Maison des Arts Georges Pompidou, Cajarac-Lot;
Ribe Kunst Museum;
Michael Werner Gallery, Cologne;
Arken Museum for Moderne Kunst, Ishøj;
BAWAG-Foundation, Vienna

1996/7
St Louis Art Museum

1997
LA Louver, Venice, California;
Dallas Museum of Art

List of exhibits

Unless otherwise indicated, all works belong to private collectors, to the artist or to Galerie Michael Werner, Cologne and New York.

Measurements are given in centimetres (height, width, depth), followed by inches in brackets

South Duveen

1 *Torso I*, 1983
Bronze patinated, edition 6+0, cast 4/6
201 x 130 x 58 (79^1/$_4$ x 51^1/$_4$ x 22^3/$_4$)

2 *Torso II*, 1983
Bronze patinated, edition 6+0, cast 2/6 196 x 122 x 48
(77^1/$_4$ x 48 x 19)

3 *Two Arms*, 1984
Bronze, edition 6, cast 3/6
77 x 86 x 89 (30^1/$_4$ x 33^3/$_4$ x 35)

4 *Large Nose*, 1984
Bronze, edition 6+0, cast 3/6
64 x 67 x 37 (25^1/$_4$ x 26^1/$_2$ x 14^1/$_2$)

5 *Head and Arm*, 1984
Bronze, edition 6+0
85 x 67 x 76 (33^1/$_2$ x 26^1/$_2$ x 30)

6 *Large Head*, 1984
Bronze, edition 6+0, cast 3/6
97 x 93 x 69 (18^1/$_4$ x 36^1/$_2$ x 27^1/$_4$)

7 *Gate I*, 1987
Bronze patinated, edition 6+0, cast 2/6
220 x 150 x 75 (86^1/$_2$ x 59 x 29^1/$_2$)

8 *Gate II*, 1987
Bronze patinated, edition 6+0, cast 4/6
240 x 170 x 60 (94^1/$_2$ x 67 x 23^1/$_2$)

9 *Torso–Branch*, 1988
Bronze patinated, edition 6, cast 1/6
220 x 144 x 60 (86^1/$_2$ x 56^3/$_4$ x 23^1/$_2$)

10 *Torso–Offshoot*, 1988
Bronze patinated, edition 6, cast 1/6
220 x 160 x 150 (86^1/$_2$ x 63 x 59)

11 *Untitled*, 1991–2
Bronze 370 x 230 x 80
(145^3/$_4$ x 90^1/$_2$ x 31^1/$_2$)

Sackler Octagon

12 *Model for Mönchengladbach*, 1985
Bronze, edition 6+0, cast 2/6
4 x 20 x 19 (1^1/$_2$ x 7^3/$_4$ x 7^1/$_2$)

13 *Model for Rijksmuseum Kröller Müller, Otterlo*, 1987
Bronze, edition 6, cast 1/6
20 x 28 x 9 (7^3/$_4$ x 10 1^1/$_4$ x 3^1/$_2$)

14 *Model for Bremen*, 1988
Bronze, edition 6, cast 1/6
35 x 15 x 13 (13^3/$_4$ x 6 x 5)

15 *Model for Amsterdam*, 1989
Bronze, edition 6
19 x 27 x 20 (7^1/$_2$ x 10^3/$_4$ x 7^3/$_4$)

16 *Model for València*, 1989
Bronze 13 x 28.5 x 26
(5 x 11^1/$_4$ x 10^1/$_4$)

17 *Model for Vevey*, 1990
Bronze, edition 6
11 x 25 x 25 (4^1/$_4$ x 9^3/$_4$ x 9^3/$_4$)

18 *Model*, 1990
Bronze, edition 6
18 x 21.5 x 18 (7 x 8^1/$_2$ x 7)

19 *Model for Års*, 1990
Bronze, edition 6
4.5 x 16 x 17 (1^3/$_4$ x 6^1/$_4$ x 6^3/$_4$)

20 *2nd Design Groningen*, undated/ca. 1990
Bronze, edition 6, cast 1/6
33.5 x 36 x 27 (13^3/$_4$ x 13 x 10^1/$_4$)

21 *Model*, 1990
Bronze, edition 6
12 x 19 x 19 (4^3/$_4$ x 7^1/$_2$ x 7^1/$_2$)

22 *Model*, 1990
Bronze, edition 6
5 x 18 x 18 (2 x 7 x 7)

23 *Model for Nakskov*, 1991
Bronze, edition 6
9 x 27 x 25 (3^1/$_2$ x 10^3/$_4$ x 9^3/$_4$)

24 *Model*, 1991
Bronze, edition 6
25 x 11 x 13 (9^3/$_4$ x 4^1/$_2$ x 5)

25 *Model for Paderborn*, 1992
Bronze, edition 6
37.5 x 31 x 10.5 (14³/₄ x 12¹/₄ x 4¹/₄)

26 *Model for Antwerp*, 1992
Bronze, edition 6
12 x 33 x 23 (4³/₄ x 13 x 9)

27 *Model for Nordland*, 1992
Bronze, edition 6
29 x 30 x 26 (11¹/₂ x 11³/₄ x 10¹/₄)

28 *Model for Göppingen*, 1992
Bronze, edition 6
11.5 x 26.5 x 13.5 (4¹/₂ x 10¹/₂ x 5¹/₄)

29 *Model for Ballerup*, 1992
Bronze patinated 16 x 33 x 8
(6¹/₄ x 13 x 3¹/₄)

30 *Model*, 1993
Bronze, edition 6
9 x 24 x 19 (3¹/₂ x 9¹/₂ x 7¹/₂)

31 *Model*, 1993
Bronze, edition 6
13 x 13 x 13 (5 x 5 x 5)

North Duveen

32 *Untitled*, 1984
Oil on canvas 300 x 400
(118 x 157¹/₂)
Museum Ludwig, Cologne,
Collection Ludwig

33 *Untitled*, 1986
Oil on canvas 300 x 350
(118 x 137³/₄)

34 *The Siege of Constantinople*, 1995
Oil on canvas 400 x 340
(157¹/₂ x 133³/₄)

35 *Flight to Egypt*, 1996
Oil on canvas 196.9 x 227.3
(77¹/₂ x 89¹/₂)
Courtesy of LA Louver Gallery,
Venice, CA

36 *Untitled*, 1997
Oil on canvas 300 x 300 (118 x 118)

37 *Withdrawn from the World*, 1997
Oil on canvas 300 x 500
(118 x 196³/₄)

38 *Brick Work*, 1998
Brick 4 x 27.7 x 2.6 metres
(13 x 88¹/₂ x 8¹/₂ feet)
Installation for the Tate Gallery
Per Kirkeby
3 February – 26 May 1998

All the following works are by
Per Kirkeby. Plates 1 and 2 are not
exhibited. For full captions of exhibited
works see list beginning on page 31.

All reproductions unless otherwise
stated, or unless photographed
in the Tate Gallery are by courtesy
of Galerie Michael Werner, Cologne
and New York.

Plate 1 *Untitled*, 1977. Oil on canvas. (Photo Lars Bay)

Plate 2 *Looking Back III*, 1987. Oil on canvas.

Plate 3   *Untitled*, 1984   (no.32)

Plate 4   *Untitled*, 1986 (no.33)

Plate 5 *The Siege of Constantinople*, 1995 (no.34)

Plate 6   *Flight to Egypt*, 1996 (no.35)

Plate 7 *Untitled*, 1997 (no.36)

Plate 8 *Withdrawn from the World*, 1997 (no.37)

Plate 9 *Torso I*, 1988. Bronze patinated (no.1)

Plate 10 *Torso II*, 1983. Bronze patinated (no.2)

Plate 11 *Large Head*, 1984. Bronze (no.6)

Plate 12 *Gate I*, 1987. Bronze patinated (no.7)

Plate 13 *Gate II*, 1987. Bronze patinated (no.8)

Plate 14 *Torso – Branch*, 1988. Bronze patinated (no.9)

Plate 15 *Torso – Offshoot*, 1988. Bronze patinated (no.10)

Plate 16 *Untitled*, 1991–2. Bronze (no.11)

Per Kirkeby in the Tate during the building of his *Brick Work*, 1998

Plates 17, 18, 19 *Brick Work*, 1998. Brick.
Installation for the Tate Gallery (no.38)

Plate 18, Plate 19 overleaf (no.38)